AF265926

From the inside out

A Look Into Teen Violence and Rebellion

By

Larry L. Stevenson

This book is a work of fiction. Places, events, and situations in this story are purely fictional. Any resemblance to actual persons, living or dead, is coincidental.

© 2003 by Larry L. Stevenson. All rights reserved.

No part of this book may be reproduced, stored in a retrieval system, or transmitted by any means, electronic, mechanical, photocopying, recording, or otherwise, without written permission from the author.

ISBN: 1-4107-3613-X (e-book)
ISBN: 1-4107-3612-1 (Paperback)

Library of Congress Control Number: 2003093622

This book is printed on acid free paper.

Printed in the United States of America
Bloomington, IN

1stBooks - rev. 07/14/03

This book is dedicated to my Lord and Savior, Jesus Christ, who entrusted me with his vision and wrote this book through me. Thank you Jesus

Special thanks goes to my wife and sons. Thank you, for your love, support and patients. God bless you.

Love-U-Me.

Contents

All scripture quotations are taken from the King James Version (KJV) also the New International Version (NIV) of the bible. Unless otherwise noted.

Today's Youth

Today is Wednesday November 21st approximately 9:35pm I just finished watching another newscast about a teen being killed by another teen. These days the violence isn't limited by race, age, or geographic area (neighborhood). As I watched this newscast, my heart went out to the victim's family because their child did not have to die in a senseless act of violence (shooting). This could have been prevented years ago. At the end of the newscast, they said a meeting would be held at the neighborhood high school to discuss how to make the neighborhood safe. This baffles me, because I can't figure out for the life of me how we can take on the challenge of making a neighborhood safe when some of us can't even manage our own homes.

I'll let you in on a little secret: If your home isn't safe, the neighborhood will never be safe. When this meeting took place I wonder who came? Parents, kids, police officers, officials, the media, and people who just wanted to be heard. Believe me I applaud your efforts, but I think if we really want to solve the problem of youth violence we must stop pointing fingers, be slow to speak and quick to listen, let down our personal walls so we can see ourselves clearly. I dare you to take a deep inward look and really ask yourself, "Am I a positive influence on my own child? Am I the person my son or daughter calls a role model, or do they look to some thug with a gift or a talent and a million dollar contract who doesn't deserve their admiration?" **WHO IS YOUR CHILD'S ROLE MODEL????**

How can we talk about making our neighborhoods safe and our own homes aren't safe? In too many families, Mommy and Daddy pay the bills, but the kids run the house! They make the decisions about whether or not they'll eat meals with the family and when they'll come home at night—if they come home at all. It's gotten to the point where parents have to knock on the child's door in your own house to see if they'll allow you to speak with them or enter their room. They make life or death decisions depending upon if they feel disrespected or not both inside and outside the home.

When we want to change the neighborhood, we tend to look at someone or something else instead of looking in the mirror. When will we realize that an external situation will only change if we make the internal changes first. If you cut your skin with a knife, that cut must begin healing through a process that takes place deep on the inside. When a body builder firms up his muscles, we know he's a body builder because we see the external difference produced by internal changes. If you're a Christian the only way your external daily walk can change is by renewing your internal thoughts, which then manifest themselves through your external actions.

Some of us will join a neighborhood meeting and know in our hearts that we left the neighborhood menace at home—the very person who can truly give us the insight on what needs to be done. We leave them at home or out running the street on purpose, fearing if we take them to the meeting they might say Mommy and Daddy are the root cause to their actions. "Mommy and Daddy don't act this concerned about me at home. They're to busy with their careers, churches, and clubs to pay attention to me. "Mommy and Daddy are to busy beating me for their mistakes instead of praising me for my progress."

I understand that bad things happen to good people, and I praise you parents who are truly trying and forgiving seventy times seven. I praise the fine, upstanding parents and citizens whose children fall to peer pressure and the ignorance of the streets. But as we look at these situations, we still need to first look inside the house and see what is being funneled in by means of TV, radio, video games, and the Internet. Each of these vehicles can influence our children in a negative way. And don't say "these things can't make that sort of negative impact on our kids" but at the same time believe these very same things can have a positive impact. If it can do the one, it most certainly can do the other.

After horrendous situations we all rush to community meetings, we rush to church to fellowship with our brothers and sisters, and we leave our homes neglected. We won't take our kids to the community meeting for fear they might blow our cover, but we force them to attend church when they don't want to go. Are you so busy and high minded that you force church down their throats, not thinking for one minute that maybe their spirit has discerned something about that particular church or pastor that you aren't willing to accept? Maybe you think you know best, because it's your church and pastor, you've been there for years and you're still wandering in the wilderness—so how could your child discern anything when he doesn't even like going to church? Remember, our children are pure at heart until we teach them differently. So when you question that child about why he doesn't want to attend church, ask yourself: What part have I played in his not wanting to go?" Have you forced your views on your son or daughter?

Whenever you force something, damage is done. Has your child discerned something about who is leading you and doesn't want to be led by the same person, place or thing that's leading you? I heard Bishop T.D. Jakes say, "be careful what you let lead you."

I'm amazed at the things people say in community meetings and gatherings. For instance, one of the first things everyone says is, "Let's start a foundation." Nine times out of ten this never comes to fruition, because people are just talking to hear themselves talk. But why say such a thing to a family that is going though one of the most tragic situations they might ever face, knowing full well you have no intention of following through?

I say, "Woe be it unto you if you make a false promise to someone in a tragic situation, trying to consol them, but have no intention of following through with your promise. If your words are found to be idle you'll have to account for those words. Woe be it unto you if our Heavenly Father finds you could have followed through with your promise and saved the life of a child of GOD!"

As I stated earlier, before we *can* change a community, first we have to change the home. I'll let you in on another little secret: If you take care of home, the community is automatically taken care of. This reminds me of the scriptures, where we're told that doing two things will take care of all ten commandments. It seems the human race couldn't master all ten commandments after Moses received them from God, so God sent Jesus to help us. When asked "Teacher, which is the greatest commandment in the Law?"

Jesus replied: "Love the Lord your God with all your heart and with all your soul and with all your mind. This is the first and greatest commandment. And the second is like it: Love your neighbor as yourself. All the Law and the Prophets hang on these two commandments." Matthew 22:36-40 NIV.

By following these two commandments, you automatically accomplish all ten!

Now that we're ready to clean up are own mess, let's look at our homes. As parents we need to understand that we're servants, leaders, and centurions at the same time, all the time. We need to be as humble servants, strong willed leaders, and filled with faith as the centurion soldier who came to Jesus and said, "Lord, my servant lieth at home sick of the palsy, grievously tormented. And Jesus saith unto him, I will come and heal him. The centurion answered and said, Lord, I am not worthy that thou shouldest come under my roof: but speak the word only, and my servant shall be healed. For I am a man under authority, having soldiers under me: and I say to this *man,* Go, and he goeth; and to another, Come, and he cometh; and to my servant, Do this, and he doeth *it.* When Jesus heard *it,* he marveled, and said to them that followed, Verily I say unto you, I have not found so great faith, no, not in Israel." Matthew 8:6-10 KJV.

I'm talking about parents who are humble enough to listen, discipline, take criticism, fix what's broken, take control of yourself, control your child, build trust both ways, and most of all be the type of parent your child can come to and talk with. Your children should feel safe enough to approach you about what's going on in their lives and know they'll receive godly counsel. How will they know this? Because they've seen you praying, they've knelt with you in prayer, and they know you've been interceding with God for your family. They come for answers because they know you have them. They don't need to look for answers out in the street or look to someone their age who's just as lost as they are. That would be like a drunk asking a wine-o how to stop drinking, while he's at the bar ordering a drink!

When we as adults are ready to take a stand and take control of our homes we need to first examine how we lead our own lives and how our children perceive us.

Now this is when it gets a little bumpy, because we don't like anyone to say negative things about us. It might be okay for them to think it to themselves, but they'd better not say it where we can hear. Here's my answer to this: In looking at ourselves and cleaning our own closets of the mind and heart, I suggest you sit in front of a mirror and talk to God (and yourself) out loud. Don't hold anything back—get all the pent up stuff you've been storing for years. Let it all hang out! Ask God for forgiveness as you hand all that crap over to him, and don't forget to say "thank you".

The hard part of this whole cleaning process is saying this stuff out loud. It's funny how our minds work. We may know and think about all our faults and the negative things we've done in life, but the minute we verbalize these negative things we try to sugar coat them, or not tell the whole truth, or fool ourselves. Do you know that a half truth is a whole lie? Sometimes we get so prideful that we can't even be alone with ourselves and speak the truth to ourselves without offending ourselves. I'm not God, a doctor, or a scientist so I can't tell you why the brain works this way, but I will tell you what happened when I started cleaning my own mind and heart closet. I sat in front of the mirror, and the moment I opened my mouth and spoke the truth about myself for the first time, I looked at me looking back at me and said "Boy if you were somebody on the street right now we'd be rolling in the dirt. How dare you talk about me like that?" I couldn't believe I was stomping on my own feelings, but at the same time I immediately felt better. The more I talked to God out loud, the better I felt inside. As I felt better inside, this had a direct effect on how I handled things with my family. I felt like I'd just taken a drink from the fountain of youth. Not only did I feel more alive, but this cleaning process took me back to things I'd gone through in my childhood that I'd never gotten off my chest or never really analyzed. Jesus said, "Larry you didn't drink from the fountain of youth, but you did get a taste of the living water." Thank You Jesus!

As you pass through this cleansing process of your mind and surroundings, God will ask you to look at your support system of people. Keep in mind that a support system is something that holds you up and can potentially help you reach the next level, not keep you on the same level or hold you back from a rewarding outcome. At this point, if you're truly listening to God, He may show you that the people around you aren't good for you. He may ask you to leave them. God will ask a woman to leave a man, or a man to leave a woman. I'm not talking about you married folks in this particular case, so don't get happy and use this as an excuse to leave your spouse. No, I'm talking about you folks who are living together, not married, and wondering why you still feel alone, discouraged, and needy. The question is—do you trust God enough to move when He says move?

"Peter said to him, "We have left everything to follow you!"

"I tell you the truth," Jesus replied, "no one who has left home or brothers or sisters or mother or father or children or fields for me and the gospel will fail to receive a hundred times as much in this present age (homes, brothers, sisters, mothers, children and fields—and with them, persecutions) and in the age to come, eternal life." Matthew 10:28-30 NIV.

One of the biggest lies, I've heard told on God by people who are living in sin and those who support them is, "we're already married in

Gods eyes." What kind of bleep, bleep, bleep is this? Where does it say in the Bible that it's acceptable to live in sin? Someone please show me, because I must have been given the wrong Bible.

Whenever you cleanse and detoxify your body, you must first take in something that causes your body to start getting rid of the toxins and waste that has been stored up and lying dormant. Once this supplement enters your system, the body begins ridding itself of toxic waste. This is similar to the process you will go through when cleansing and detoxifying (renewing) your mind. First, you get the spirit of truth down inside you. Once this happens, your mind will start to rid itself of all the toxic waste of the flesh that has been stored up for years. As this process gets underway, God will show you things about yourself, family, friends and church that are not of the spirit. If you're one of those people who believe just because you have a child with someone and live with them you're married in God's eyes, let me be the first to tell you the truth. You are living in sin, fornicating, and raising another generation that will continue to live this lie and carry this curse!

God will show you a motion picture of your life through your past thoughts and actions, he will start to question you on your life. Keep in mind that when God asks a question he already knows the answer. This is simply apart of the cleansing process. I believe he wants to see if you're going to be honest with him. He'll ask things such as, "How can you tell your child not to drink when you drink? How can you tell your child not to smoke when you smoke? How can you tell your child not to cuss when you cuss? How can you tell your child not to lie when you lie? How can you talk to your children about the company they keep when your friends are just as bad?"

You tell your children not to do all the above thing, but you don't practice what you preach. I'm not talking about not doing these things around them—I'm talking about giving them up and over to God. What's more important: your healthy child or your filthy habits? Most adults will make the excuse "I'm grown" and use this to support their bad habits. This is one of the lamest excuses in the book. What makes you grown—your age or your mind set? Believe me if you're still doing these things, saying one thing and doing another, you haven't put away childish things! How can you tell children to keep their rooms clean when yours is dirty? So what if you're grown and pay the bills? Parenthood is about teaching correct principles and setting a positive example. Most of all, how can you tell your children they need Jesus, when you don't have Jesus in your own life. As a parent, you need Jesus twice as much as they do—for yourself and to help you raise your child.

You tell them to go to bed at a certain time, but you don't come home until the wee hours of the morning. You tell them to read the Bible, but they don't see you reading it. Sure they see it around the house and you might carry it with you, but they don't see you reading and studying. Try this during your reading of the Bible: read it aloud where everyone in your home can hear you and watch the spirit of God work. God said that his word "shall not return to him void." Read His word so everyone can hear, and your family will experience a mighty movement of the spirit.

Please understand that whatever instructions you give your children, you follow the same rules. If you tell them not to dress like a thug make sure you pull your own pants up around your waist, or wear skirts that cover your thighs. If you tell them not to gossip about others, keep your own speech motivating, positive, and uplifting and be slow to speak and quick to listen. If you tell them not to have premarital sex, you shouldn't it either. If you tell your children to respect their elders, then you must respect your peers, elders, and children.

14

The Problem is in the Solution

Most people realize that whenever there's a problem, the solution is hidden within that same problem. In most cases, this is true. However when we look at teen violence and rebellion we must take the unique approach: The problem is in the solution! For example: Your teen is out of control. As a solution, you put them on a talk show for supposed help and advice, but all you're really doing is promoting more rebellion. Is this the answer? No!

Another problem might be a teen who's violent and out of control. As a solution, you send them to boot camp where they learn a few things, and maybe change their behavior. Unfortunately, once they return home to you they go back to their old ways, because they're thrust back into the same environment that contributed to the original problem. The problem here is that someone should've sent you to boot camp at the same time your child went there. Is this the answer? Not until we get a boot camp for adults. It does no good for your child to change, if your attitude and actions remain the same. Remember they are mimicking you!

"Neither do men pour new wine into old wineskins. If they do, the skins will burst, the wine will run out and the wineskins will be ruined. No, they pour new wine into new wineskins, and both are preserved." Matthew 9:17 NIV.

When attempting to solve a problem, we must first look at ourselves and make sure we don't have anything in our present lives that might hinder or curse our efforts in fact finding.

"Why do you look at the speck of sawdust in your brother's eye and pay no attention to the plank in your own eye? How can you say to your brother, 'Let me take the speck out of your eye,' when all the time there is a plank in your own eye? You hypocrite, first take the plank out of your own eye, and then you will see clearly to remove the speck from your brother's eye." Matthew 7:3-5

Please understand that I'm not just talking about cleaning up our own lives, but also making sure the person, place, or thing to which we turn for help is producing good fruit. You must sow your confidence into good ground!

Yes I'm talking about your mother, your father, the pastor, your boyfriend, your girlfriend and every other person in whom you confide when you face a struggle or attempt to straighten out your life. Do you ever wonder why every time you attempt to do better in life and reach out to a certain person for encouragement and help, you always end up back where you started? This is called "back sliding" The reason people continue to back slide is because they never renew their minds with a complete overhaul, they never fully complete the cleansing process by extending it to their surroundings.

Let us look at some of the things we never do: First, we never really admit our own problems, but instead chalk things up to "that's how I was raised." Just because you were brought up a certain way is no excuse for bad behavior. You need to take a look at your childhood and see what negative things you've brought forward to the future of your life. How do these attitudes affect the way you raise your child? What you are letting your children get away with because you were raised that way? How are you treating them because you were raised that way? For example, suppose you were raised in a house where your mother or father constantly degraded whatever you attempted to do put you down as a person. Why would you want to raise your own child like that? Why would you want to put your own child down and kill his self esteem or self image and push him away so he has to seek the love of a gang or feel the constant need to prove his self worth?

Folks, it's time to wake up and do your own background check instead of trying to do one on these young folks. Believe me, whatever is in your background caught a one way non-stop generational flight, straight to your child's emotions.

Many people continue back sliding because of the company they keep. We as people over the years have fallen into this rut of not telling the truth, to others or ourselves. Ask yourself, why are you trying to change your life, but continuing to confide in and rely on people who are worse off than you are? For example, if you're beating or cheating on your spouse, why would you call someone you know who's doing the same thing and ask them for advice. Do not laugh; do not frown. This really happens. What I am saying is: If you truly want to change for the better, then you must stop confiding in people who will just go with the flow of what you're saying or doing. You need to find a new source of support, someone who's headed down the path you want to travel. This means that if you're the type of person who runs to their parents for guidance when things go wrong, you need to first take a close look at your parents and how they handle their own problems. Just because they're your parents doesn't mean they'll give you sound advice. If the advice is not sound: Do you really want that kind of advice? And if you already know what they'll say to you, then why confide in them anyway? I will tell you why: Because when people are searching for a solution to their problem, they won't go to someone who will be open and honest with them and tell them the truth, even if it hurts. No, people seek out those who'll tell them what they want to hear, or someone who'll just listen to them vent without offering advice. Basically most people seek someone who will make them feel good instead of someone who cares about their greater good.

The same goes for people who run to the church and seek the pastor's help because you want to get out of your fleshly rut. In order for this pastor to be of some assistance to you, you have to *want* to change. You must believe that your pastor has been interceding with God on your behalf and will speak the word of God in and over your situation. Believe me when I tell you your flesh hates your spirit because "the mind is willing, but the flesh is weak," and you know it's in our nature to hate anything stronger then us. That's why there is a constant war between the flesh and the spirit, because the flesh hates that the spiritual mind is stronger. Your mind focuses on completing whatever you put in it. If the thought is negative, it will go with that, but if the thought is positive it will try to complete that. Scripture says

"For as he thinketh in his heart, so *is* he". Proverbs 7 KJV.

I know some of you may be thinking that if you start confiding in sources other than your usual ones for help then someone's feelings might get hurt. So what! You just might get them to rethink their own situation. Tom Robbins said, "Real courage is risking something that might force you to rethink your thoughts and suffer change and stretch consciousness." Take it from me, if you keep going to the same old source and you know their own life is in disarray, then you really are "killing two birds with one stone." You're literally killing both of your chances for immediate change by being selfish and just wanting to be pacified by another instead of healed by a truly spiritual sister or brother.

This whole time we've concentrated on the people in our lives when seeking a solution. But please understand that as long as you seek a solution before you seek God, then your problem will always be in the solution. That's because even if you are seeking advice from a godly person, you may not be able to hear and interpret what God is saying through this person, because you put that person before God.

God said "There will be no other gods before him and seek ye first the kingdom of heaven and all these things will be provided unto you". He did not say "except for your momma and them!" Excuse my Ebonics (smile).

I always tell the people whom I have the privilege of ministering to, that if they have a situation in their lives and they're seeking help or answers, "Don't call me before you talk to God, because the only answers I have to offer you are godly answers. But until you've talked to God you won't be able to hear Him speak through me to you." If you seek a man's opinion first, you'll receive a man's answer. If any one gives you counsel other than godly counsel, you shouldn't want it anyway. I am a firm believer that you seek God first and talk to him before you drive over to the pastor's house of call Sally, Suzie, or Mary. God will give you an answer which will be confirmed by the source you seek, after you've have spoken with God first.

Many times people have called me concerned about something in their lives, and my first question to them is always, "Have you talked to God about this?" If the answer is no, I let them know in a nice way that the conversation is over! I tell them to call back after they've spoken to God. Once the conversation between them and God takes place, we can move ahead from there, because now they can hear Him speaking through me. They will be able to discern my fleshly thoughts and comments from the spiritual and receive divine direction, along with that small quiet voice inside them (the Holy Spirit) telling them which way to turn.

Jesus said, "My sheep hear my voice, and I know them, and they follow me." John 10:27 KJV.

Ocean of emotions

Have you ever walked into a room and said to yourself "This room has no energy?" Or you've thought, "I can feel the energy in this room." Have you ever entered a room and felt your energy being sapped away? This is called the transference of energy. Sir Isaac Newton said, "Energy is neither lost nor destroyed, it's merely transferred from one party to the next."

Our emotions can effect a room full of people. With that in mind, we really need to get a handle on the emotions we develop in and bring to our homes. Let's face it, as adults in our homes we are the main focal point, a centerpiece in our children's lives. In our homes our kids feel the good, the bad, and the ugly part of our emotions whenever they're around us. We can literally walk into our houses and change the atmosphere without saying a word. It's up to you whether the atmosphere inside your home is positive or negative.

Am I saying you can't or won't have a bad day? No! But I am saying that when these days come you should take the mind set of David and tell yourself "This is the day the Lord has made, I will rejoice and be glad in it." Remind yourself that your wife, husband, mother, father or boss did not make this day. The Lord himself designed and gift-wrapped this day just for you, and you should not frown upon a gift from God. Because how you act during these so-called bad days and how you finish scene one, act one determines whether your character gets a standing ovation or booed off the stage. Pray for what has taken you out of the spirit, hand it over to God, and believe that while you're praying God is literally right there with you, writing all your requests down on paper with the precious blood of Jesus, so he can help you overcome this problem. Once you've finished praying, tell yourself "God is on the job." Don't try to go behind God and look over His shoulder to see how he's handling your business. Just trust that the business is being handled. What person would have the nerve to think they can micromanage God?

Believe me I'm a passionate, emotional person who's tried to handle God's business my own way, thinking I knew what was best for me at the time. Only later I would find out that I almost had the curtain pulled on my character.

When we let our emotions get the best of us around our kids, don't you think that's kind of selfish? Whether you know it or not, once you have children, life not just about you anymore. Your child feeds off your every emotion. So now think about your equalizer of emotions and ask yourself, "How much time do I spend with dangerous (angry, depressed, negative) emotions around my children?" Now, ask yourself "Why would I want to poison my child's emotions with my own garbage?" Instead, you can choose to pray on the matter or take a little mental break to regroup and then bring positive, uplifting, loving emotions to your children.

Our children have so much to deal with today in this high tech world in which we live. I say high tech because our children are walking computer chips and hard drives. It's not an overstatement to say they're downloading everything around them. And increasing memory everyday, a computer chip or hard drive never looses it's information it simply gets upgraded or updated from time to time. Haven't you ever wondered why you can be 40 years old and still be affected by something that happened when you were 5. That is because what happened back then has been stored in your hard drive and you or nobody around you ever bothered to do a virus scan, so you've been walking around for 35 years with a virus of the mind infected and infecting. Every time you open your mouth to speak is like sending an e-mail from your computer whether known or unknown you may be sending a virus, for the bible says that the power of life and death is in the tongue.

You may be thinking I'm too hard on folks, but I'm saying what no one else will say for fear of not being liked. I could easily please you by saying everything's going to be all right, getting you all happy and fired up. The problem with this kind of empty motivation is that sooner or later that wears off and we will find ourselves back in the same situation. The definition for motivate is: to provide an incentive. Once the incentive is gone, so is your motivation. Motivation is temporary. My intent is not to motivate you. My intent is to push your buttons and have you take a good look at yourself and the surroundings in which you dwell. I want you to look at the negative, think about what's wrong and how you can change it. I need you to get tired, get fed up, and come to your senses.

"Tell the devil, I changed my mind." Bishop T.D. Jakes.

I want you to feel uncomfortable while reading this book, because that means something is stirring up inside you, and if we stir something up then we know that deep down inside you want to change, you want to be different, you want something different for your family.

The definition for change is: *to cause to be different, to give a completely different form or appearance to; to transform.* This is exactly why I'm writing—to help you learn to transform your mind, your emotions, your character, and your actions. If we change all these things, we will change your home and everything in it. If we change the home, then we change the community. And once the community is changed, then we have truly effected change.

Mirror Image

Your child is a mirror image of you! Children imitate or emulate everything their parents say and do. If you don't believe me, think back to when your child was a toddler. Who did he mimic then? The same person he's mimicking today! From your best deeds to your worst habits, your children are carbon copies of you. So when your son or daughter is out there acting like a menace to society, ask yourself: In what way, shape, or form have they seen me act in a menacing or threatening manner, so they thought it was okay to behave that way? Just because you don't carry a gun or knife doesn't mean you don't act in a menacing manner. Your mouth can be a gun, and your tongue a knife.

"Even so every good tree bringeth forth good fruit; but a corrupt tree bringeth forth evil fruit. A good tree cannot bring forth evil fruit, neither *can* a corrupt tree bring forth good fruit. Matt. 7:17-18 KJV.

As we look at the above quote, we need to understand that our kids are an exact replica of our own emotions and activities. What your kids see you do and hear you say is *exactly* what they'll end up doing and saying at some point in time. Children are most likely to copy their parents during two critical stages of life. The first is the infant/toddler stage, when their emotions, thoughts, and actions are very impressionable.

During this stage we adults are constantly saying to the child "do this or say this." Sometimes the things we're telling them to do or say are things we'll punish them for doing when they get older. It seems cute when they're only three years old, but the same behavior isn't so attractive in a fifteen year old. Have you ever encouraged a toddler to mimic your actions in doing a dance move that has sexual overtones, or involves touching or grabbing their sexual organs? Another example might be teaching your child to make their fingers in the form of a gun and act as though they're shooting something. During later years, you'll punish them for picking up a gun and acting out the same thing you taught them as a child.

Do you see what this action could lead to? Well, let me break it down for you. Your child could end up doing 25 years to life for murdering someone by simply carrying out the things you encouraged when they were little. Or worse, your child could be the one placed in the ground at the funeral because he or she was playing the same game as a teen they used to play as toddlers—but this time played with a real gun instead of a finger. I don't mean to alarm you or sound judgmental but this is a wake up call! You may get upset with me while reading these pages and think I'm judging the way you raise your child. But if this book causes you to do one thing differently that might save the life of a child, then get upset all you want. You'll have to admit the real reason you're upset is because I'm telling the truth when nobody else would tell you. So go ahead—get mad enough to save a life!

The second most impressionable stage in your child's life is the teenage years, because suddenly all the negative things you taught them or allowed them to get a way with will surface. Now they will push the envelope and push your buttons.

- If one or more of these things go on in your house, don't be surprised when you have problems with your children:

- Domestic acts of violence both physical and verbal

- Cussing

- Constant watching of violence

- Listening to degrading, violent, depressing music

- Lack of reassurance and affirmation

- No physical affection (a hand shake, hug or pat on the back can save a life)

- Not following through with the positive discipline and structure

And, last but not least, the giving your child to much freedom in a vain attempt to be thought of as a good parent. The book of Matthew, chapter 7 verse 11 states, "If ye then, being evil, know how to give good gifts unto your children, how much more shall your Father which is in heaven give good things to them that ask him?"

Often when we hear this scripture we automatically think of the monetary or material things we give our children. However, I believe when Jesus spoke of giving he meant whatever you give them should be of benefit to them and nothing that will harm them. This is why we need to take heed of our actions, our speaking, and our way of living, because every time your children watch you go through something you set an example for them. By watching your actions, they are asking you for direction. Through their positive and negative actions they ask for your attention. So now, think for a moment on what you've been giving them. Materially you might give your child all the gifts they ask for and believe you're correct because the scripture says:

"what man is there of you, whom if his son ask bread, will he give him a stone? Or if he ask a fish will give him a serpent? Matthew 7:9-10 KJV. However, I want to challenge you by asking this:, Do you really think Jesus was only talking about things that you can touch? I think not. Why have you been giving your children stones through you actions, instead of bread? Why have you given them serpents through your emotions, instead of fish? You might say that as a child you never received anything better, so now you don't believe your child requires anything more. Let me remind you that you're always a child of God no matter your age, no matter how grown up you think you are. You never grow old to your daddy!

The funny thing is, even when raising our children, in the back of our mind we sometimes think, "But what about me? I am giving to this child and nobody is giving to me." Let me direct you to the book of Acts 20:35, which simply states, "It is more blessed to give than to receive." I will tell you something else: If you give it, you will get it. What you sow, you will reap. "Sow a thought, and you reap an act; sow an act, and you reap a habit; sow a habit, and you reap a character; sow a character, and you reap a destiny"

What better ground to sow into then the life of your child!

The Domestic Violence Web

Did you know that domestic violence leads to teen violence?

As we look at the terrible acts of domestic violence in the world today, we must look at the snowball affect it has on our children. Think about this every time you raise your voice to your spouse, boyfriend, or girlfriend. Think about this every time you degrade them and talk about what you would or are going to do to them. This is bad enough by itself. However, these words you utter in front of your children begin or continue a generational curse. Your children store this information in their little heads and say to themselves "If I am the man in the relationship, I'm supposed to talk to my woman like that. If I'm the woman, I should let my man talk to me like this. I'm supposed to treat people like this, because that's how my mom and or dad treat each other."

This type of verbal abuse leads to another level of violence—the physical. Whether this happens with you and your loved one or not, understand that your kids always take what they see mommy and daddy doing another step further. For example, suppose your child hears Mommy and Daddy arguing and one of them threatens to physically harm the other. Your child hears this and thinks, "If it's okay to harm people within the family, it must be okay, and that much easier, to harm someone outside the family. This leads to teen violence! Violence without emotion or thought. Random acts without fear.

We adults just don't seem to get it. We don't seem to understand that every argument, every little push, every shove, every grab, every act of tit for tat is watched by children, who are taking mental notes to see how they will treat the man, woman, or child in their lives. In a sense you could call domestic violence, domestic terrorism and say that parents are the trainers and leaders of terrorist training camp inside their homes. Children who follow their parents' examples are like the next generations of terrorist training in the Al Qaeda camps. And like the Al Qaeda, your children are willing to die or kill for what they believe in, because they were raised with these rules. As long as your home is violent, your neighborhood will never be safe! Non-violent home, non-violent neighborhood! Fruitless home, fruitless neighborhood, Spirit filled home, spirit filled neighborhood.

Pray aloud

Please understand when I tell you to pray aloud, I am not saying go against scripture. Scripture tells us:

"And when thou prayest, thou shalt not be as the hypocrites *are:* for they love to pray standing in the synagogues and in the corners of the streets, that they may be seen of men. Verily I say unto you, They have their reward. But thou, when thou prayest, enter into thy closet, and when thou hast shut thy door, pray to thy Father which is in secret; and thy Father which seeth in secret shall reward thee openly." Matthew 6:5-6 KJV.

What I am asking you to do takes place in your house with your family, after you have finished interceding with God on behalf of your family in your closet. When you pray aloud with your family on bended knees or touching and agreeing with bowed heads or lifted hands, this has a huge impact on leading and teaching—not only for your children, but for you as well. Many of us like to pray silently or use a scripted prayer for fear others might judge us as we have judged them. In doing this we teach our children to be shy about their prayer life instead of outspoken. We teach them to pray scripted prayers instead of praying from their hearts. Look at what praying with your family aloud teaches you and your children. When you pray you are humbling yourself, acknowledging that you don't have all the answers, that you're not superman, but Clark Kent. You hurt and have issues just like everyone else, and when you need answers or want to get things off your chest, you don't call somebody on the phone, you don't go to talk to someone who has just as many problems as you. Instead, you call on the sum of the whole body which is the Father in the name of Jesus.

Seeing you pray also teaches your children to pray from their hearts and simply say what's on their minds instead of saying the same scripted prayer over and over. I believe by praying a scripted prayer all the time many people expect God to change their lives, but they won't take the time or effort to share with Him what's in their hearts. Although God knows your mind and what's in it, He wants to hear it in your own words. So you may blame God for not giving you something you haven't even asked for, while in actuality God is waiting on you!

"You do not have because you do not ask God." James 4:2 NIV

This piece of scripture in and of itself is a pot of gold, but if you don't examine the treasure you wont find what's buried in it. Thus, you will continue to believe you're waiting for God to read your mind.

Many times in my not so distant past I read the before mentioned scripture and said to myself, "I've been asking but I haven't been receiving" When in fact I was receiving, but not on the level I expected. Later I realized that although I asked God for certain things, there was something missing on my end of the deal. It wasn't until New Years Eve of this past year that I found out what was missing. My family and I were at watch night service and Pastor Gary Bagwell spoke about being specific when asking God to bless you. He referred to two key scriptures: Mark 10:46-52, and 1 kings 3:5-10. In both scriptures the Lord is asking a man what is it he would have the Lord do for him.

This really speaks to us folks who always preach the message of the Lord knowing our hearts. Yes, he does know our hearts, but he also created us with free will, so our hearts may want one thing, while our minds and mouths say something totally different. Therefore God gave us these important scriptures about asking for what we want and being specific about what we're asking for. For example, many of us ask God to bless are finances. Suppose in January you asked God to bless your finances, and here it is December 31st and you only received a 25 cent raise for the year. Another year passed and your finances and are no better. You're still singing that same old sad song about just waiting on the Lord. The problem is, if you want God to bless your finances, then ask for the specific amount you need. Just ask Him. He wants to bless you, but he also wants to know what's in your heart.

So when you're teaching your children to pray, show them by example how to be specific and talk to God from the heart. Also, I can't stress this enough: Whenever you're speaking God's word aloud He promises his word will not return unto him void. So while you're praying for your child you should be able to touch on their situation and not even know it by simply speaking the word of God and praying in the spirit.

By praying aloud you not only lead your family, but you teach your children how to be humble, how to simply talk to God, how to pray *for* and not *about* others, how to first seek the council of God before man, and how to lead their families and effect the next generation.

Listen to the listening

What are your kids hearing you say, and more importantly—what are they watching you do? What do your body language and actions say to them? What are your voice tones telling them? Do you laugh at serious situations when directing your children, fearing that if you use a serious, stern voice they might get mad at you and not be your friend anymore? You might laugh at this but it's exactly how some parents act these days! News flash, Folks: you are the parents! You need to raise them first, and then you can look at a friendship. You need to be a father or a mother with a friendly side to you, but as far as becoming your child's homie, girlfriend, partner, or running buddy you need to save that for when they're grown and out on their own. We let friends get away with things we should call them on, we let friendship blind us to facts, and sometimes a friendship can ruin a relationship. We don't want anything getting in the way of raising our children properly. When we begin to befriend our children and hear certain things from folks outside the home about something our child may have done, we start to say things like My child wouldn't do that.". So why not just stick to positive parenting instead of false friendships?

When you "listen to the listening," first you must give verbal instructions, and then you listen to the response and watch future actions, which are the outcomes of your instructions. For example, perhaps you instruct your child to come straight home after the school dance and the dance is over at 10:00 P.M. He arrives home a little after 10, but later you find he left the dance at 8P.M. and went to hang out at a house party, or rode around visiting friends. Is your child wrong, or did you not listen to the listening?

You did say to come straight home after the dance, which is what your son did. What your child heard you say is, You can hang out, as long as you're home right around 10P.M.

How could you have let him understand *exactly* what you meant? By saying, "Once you leave the dance, come straight home." This way, both of you understand the rules.

When it comes to raising children, our communication should be clear, concise, and without question. Then they don't come back and say, "I thought you meant such and such." When you instruct your child, what you're communicating should be a no brainer. If you watch people doing sign language the message is clear, with no hmms, uhmms or gaps. The message is straight to the point.

I spent years with my oldest son telling him the don't do's of life. "Don't do drugs, don't drink, don't drink and drive, don't do this and don't do that." Every time I told him don't do one thing, I was leaving room for him to do several other things by omission. One day we were going to the store and I said to him "Son, every time I tell you not to do something negative you don't, but then you end up doing something else negative instead. I know you're listening! Now let me ask. Do you know what a mistake is?"

"Yes," he replied.

"In that case," I said, "from now on don't make any mistakes"

Now he understood he wasn't supposed to do anything considered a mistake. The funny thing is, after that conversation he told me it was the smartest thing anyone ever said to him about doing wrong. Mother Theresa of Calcutta said it best when asked by Henri Nouwen how he should live out his vocation as a priest. She simply said "Spend one hour a day in adoration of your Lord and **never do anything you know is wrong, and you'll be all right**." Meister Eckhart.

The Holy Spirit recently imparted some knowledge in my soul about discussing and giving details of our pasts. This occurred while I watched a talk show about children who have rebelled against their parents. In one segment of the show, a grown woman came out and ran down a list of things she'd done, from drugs to sex and beyond. In the next breath she stated how after experiencing all these things in the past, she's now doing well now. This is when the Holy Spirit showed me another way of thinking and listening. As I considered it, I remembered some of my talks with my kids and how I would run down the list of my wrong doings as if to glorify them. I was saying, "Just look at me now!" I remember hearing preachers who speak from the pulpit about how bad they were in the past—and they're also saying, "Look at me now!" Do you see what we're doing when we say these things? More importantly, do you hear what your kids are hearing when you give a detailed account of all the wrong in your past and how great you're doing now? They don't need details! I know in saying this some people will say "Don't forget where you came from" but there are things in your past we can and should forget.

When your child hears you telling them all your dirt, they hear a completely different meaning then you expect. You tell them that you used to be in a gang, you used to sell drugs, you used to drink to get drunk, you used to sleep with any and everybody, and the list goes on. Your trying to make a point of "been there, done that" and you hope they see you're a changed person, doing much better now. And if you can change, anybody can change. Or if God saved you, He will save anybody! But guess what your children are hearing you say? For the most part they hear it's okay and borderline cool **to do** all the negative they want, because they'll grow out of it or God will save them from it. "You can do it, go through it, and live to tell about it."

So I want you to understand that your child doesn't need to hear the negative things you've done, even if you were in prison for some ungodly crime and are now a world-renowned preacher. They don't need details on your crime in order for you to make your point about how good life is treating you now. Instead, lead them to this scripture:

KJV 1Peter 4:12-13 Beloved, think it not strange concerning the fiery trial which is to try you, as though some strange thing happened unto you: But rejoice, inasmuch as ye are partakers of Christ's sufferings; that, when his glory shall be revealed, ye may be glad also with exceeding joy.

KJV 1Corithians 10:13 There hath no temptation taken you but such as is common to man: but God *is* faithful, who will not suffer you to be tempted above that ye are able; but will with the temptation also make a way to escape, that ye may be able to bear *it.*

This scripture reassures your children that they'll never be tempted above what they can handle, and God always provides a way to escape temptation. The way out is through Christ, not through friends, parents, preachers or teachers. For the scripture says, "I can do all things through Christ that strengthens me."

Prevention = Promotion

During the 80's there was a saying that "Gang prevention equals gang promotion." This means that the preventive efforts practiced at home, in the community, in the schools, and through the media, actually promote gangs.

Think about it this way: Whenever a violent act, uprising, or negative issue with children occurs, we can hardly wait to put it in the public eye through the media. Then this issue becomes a household topic of discussion for an extended period. The perpetrators get lots of attention and notoriety, as do the victims.

On the other hand, when a child finally gets a job, brings home good grades, or turns the other cheek and chooses not to fight, there's no visible reward. Our focus is always on the negative, and our children see this. They realize that doing wrong will gain them not only attention from their parents, but also local or national media attention.

Most people believe you're supposed to have long, drawn out conversations with your children when they do something negative.

Well, why not spend quality time with them when they do something positive? Why not hug them and tell them how proud and thankful you are to God that He gave them as a gift to you? If you don't do this, then your children get more affection and human contact from you when you talk at them in the negative and spank or slap them then they get when they do something positive. Knowing this, wouldn't you do wrong too?

I'm asking you to change your focus. I'm asking you to sacrifice that feeling deep in the pit of your belly, or the nagging feeling buried in the recesses of your mind that has held you and your family back. I'm asking you to sacrifice that *on guard* feeling, for the peace that passes all understanding! All these feelings have been telling you to try a different approach. What can it hurt? The way you've been going hasn't worked thus far, so why not try the righteous approach? Scripture tells us that one person can save a whole family. The LORD then said to Noah, "Go into the ark, you and your whole family, because I have found you righteous in this generation. Genesis 7:1 NIV.

If one person can change a family, and then a family can save a neighborhood, then that's a start. You must understand that something has to change, because if you keep doing what you're doing you will keep getting what you're getting. What will it cost if you don't change your focus and you keep up your fleshly ways? It will cost your inheritance! "Now the works of the flesh are manifest, which are these; Adultery, fornication, uncleanness, lasciviousness, Idolatry, witchcraft, hatred, variance, emulations, wrath, strife, seditions, heresies, Envyings, murders, drunkenness, revellings, and such like: of the which I tell you before, as I have also told you in time past, that they which do such things **shall not inherit** the kingdom of God. But the fruit of the Spirit is love, joy, peace, longsuffering, gentleness, goodness, faith, Meekness, temperance: against such there is no law. Galatians 5:19-23 KJV.

As brother, Jesse Duplantis would say, "Don't shout me down when I'm preaching good."

Step Parents

The role of the step parent has been scrutinized and judged for years, and has often received a bad rap from those of us who are the actual stepparents. I want to tell you my own story of how God opened my eyes and convicted me so badly I had to humble myself and seek forgiveness from my two step-sons.

I have been part of my stepson's lives for about 8 years; I married their mother in June of '99. Although they accepted me as their father, I in my worldly, stupid, stubborn way of thinking could not get past the *step* part of the father role. I felt the word *step* automatically put me second, and their *real* father would ultimately overturn my role in their lives. I told myself, if my wife and I ever divorced there would be no problem, because ultimately these kids had a birth father. How stupid could I be? Let me answer that for you: very stupid! This type of thinking led to a nonchalant attitude when it came to what was best for the kids, and had a direct effect on my actions toward them. I felt I didn't have to do certain things *for* them or *with* them, because their real dad would handle these things. I found myself feeling jealous when they received a gift from their real dad, or when they called him

Dad and referred to me by my first name. I was even jealous of their

relationship with my wife, because they'd call her for permission to

go over a friend's house or make something to eat. At first, when I

was still out there in the world (being lead by my mind instead of the

spirit), I found it okay for me to drink, cuss, argue with their mom,

and hang out 'till all hours of the night with my friends. I would

promise to do something with the boys and it never come to pass, or

be so hard and judgmental on them in their school work and chores

that there was no room for error—it was either my way or no way. If I

was a typical stepfather, then it's no wonder kids can't stand their step

parents.

During the early stages of my initial cleansing process, I found

myself talking to God and asking him to bless my wife and me with a

child, so that I would have a child of my own. And then it happened.

It was like God said to me "I've been waiting for you to say

something like this, because we need to talk." God spoke clearly to

my spirit and convicted me when he said, "Larry, how can I trust you

with a child of your own when I can't trust you to be a good

stepfather?" It was as though he said, "If I can't trust you with a few things, how can I make you ruler over many things?" Then he led me to this piece of scripture in the book of Matthew:

Now the birth of Jesus Christ was on this wise: When as his mother Mary was espoused to Joseph, before they came together, she was found with child of the Holy Ghost. 19 Then Joseph her husband, being a just man, and not willing to make her a public example, was minded to put her away privily. 20 But while he thought on these things, behold, the angel of the Lord appeared unto him in a dream, saying, Joseph, thou son of David, fear not to take unto thee Mary thy wife: for that which is conceived in her is of the Holy Ghost. 21 And she shall bring forth a son, and thou shalt call his name JESUS: for he shall save his people from their sins. 22 Now all this was done, that it might be fulfilled which was spoken of the Lord by the prophet, saying, 23 Behold, a virgin shall be with child, and shall bring forth a son, and they shall call his name Emmanuel, which being interpreted is, God with us. 24 Then Joseph being raised from sleep did as the angel of the Lord had bidden him, and took unto him his wife: 25 And knew her not till she had brought forth her firstborn son: and he called his name JESUS. Matthew 1:18-25 KJV.

After I read this scripture, God told me I needed to stand where Joseph stood in his day. If you read this scripture carefully, you'll realize that ultimately Joseph was Jesus' stepfather. Once I understood this I had to fall on my knees and repent for my thoughts and actions. As the scriptures say:

"If you are offering your gift at the altar and there remember that your brother has something against you, leave your gift there in front of the altar. First go and be reconciled to your bother; then come and offer your gift." Matthew 5:23-24 NIV.

Please think hard about this. Many people who read the above scripture only think about the adults in their lives when they read the word *brother*. Rarely if at all do we think of our own children as our brothers or sisters. However, under God's care we are all brothers and sisters, because we have the same father. Although my stepsons are my sons, they are also my brothers.

After reading those scriptures and understanding what God was telling me, I had to humble myself before my sons, asking their forgiveness for the way I'd treated them. I let them know that from that moment on I would no longer refer to them as my stepsons. Now I simply call them *my sons*. I might not have made them, but today I am making, shaping, and molding them. Without blinking an eye, without 2 seconds ticking off the clock, the words, "Yes, I forgive you," came from the mouths of these children, and it was as though Jesus himself spoke through them. An overwhelming feeling of relief came over me. Our relationship has grown more in the short time since that day then it ever did over the past few years. We now do home Bible study twice a week and we pray aloud together (I want to stress the aloud because, I find when you do this Gods words do not return void). Most families won't pray out loud together because they don't feel they know how to pray correctly. But as long as you call on the Father in the name of Jesus and pray from the heart, you can't go wrong. The boys and I work out together, and we've developed what I feel is a true father son relationship. I almost forgot to mention that one of my sons calls me "Pops" and my wife and I have overheard the other one on the phone with his friends refer to me as "my dad."

Make no mistake about it: those are my babies, my boys!

The whole time I was looking at what I considered a problem—the *step* part of parenting. However, I now understand it wasn't a problem, it was a small challenge with a huge opportunity to make a world of difference in the lives of two boys. I like to think God called me to "step" into position, "step" up to the challenge and "step" into the opportunity to make a difference in a child's life.

Step up, stand up and be counted, because those children are counting on you.

You are the **Step** up **Parent,** and their lives depend on you!

Larry L. Stevenson

The Preacher's Kid

Everywhere you go, in and out of church circles there's a common theme when it comes to the preacher's kid: They're the worst of all the kids being raised in that generation. This takes me back to my own childhood. I grew up with plenty of preacher's kids (PK's). I heard people talk about how they would rebel at times and that they were worse then any of us other kids. There's a simple reason why people across the world share the same views about PKs' being so bad. It isn't really that the PK is worse then any other child in the neighborhood, it's because more people know the preachers kids because these young people are on display all the time, and people expect more from them. When your father or mother is a preacher, you're held to a higher standard than other children. For example: If a child in the congregation gets in trouble and suspended from school, nobody really comments on it. But if the preacher's kid does the exact same thing and gets suspended from school, then the child's actions will be a topic of discussion throughout the community and the congregation. We must remember when putting these children underneath the microscope that the parent was called to the ministry, but the child is still a child and has the same basic wants, needs, and issues as your child; it's just that your life may not be as public as the preacher's.

"So when they continued asking him, he lifted up himself, and said unto them, **He that is without sin among you, let him first cast a stone** at her" John 8:7 KJV

As a preacher of the gospel, one of the most important things you need in your life is not a large congregation or a huge following, but balance and knowing how to balance. This is where many preachers fall short in their callings. They tend to concentrate more on the calling than the caller. If your call is truly from God and not of man, then please tell us: Does God expect you to neglect your home in order to serve others? Unfortunately, many preachers spend more time at church functions than school functions, more time at Bible study than helping their children study, more time preaching than speaking to their own children, more time at watch night service than watching their own children at night, and more time balancing their building fund checkbook than doing the checks and balances at home. When you where called by God, did he tell you to stop spending time with your family? I've heard preachers say their children understand they have to be gone from home, evangelizing and saving souls. While you're out saving all those lost souls, who is saving your children's souls and helping them understand the word of God? Even if you spoke with them and said they understand what you have to do, they still miss having you around.

Remember when you first taught them how pray and you got so choked up when you heard those little voices say, "God bless mommy and daddy." Picture this: when those little prayers went up from the pure heart of a child and touched the heart of God, perhaps He answered that child's prayer by calling you to preach the gospel or growing your ministry beyond your wildest dreams. Yet now you don't have time to spend with the very person who made the phone call to God, and got you the job or promotion. Do you think God called you because you tell stories well, or because of the school of theology you attended, or because you where so bad in the streets that he did it to save your life? Give me a break with that self-centered nonsense! He may have called you or sustained you because your child prayed for you! However, when you tell the story, you talk about how all the church mothers and your grandmother prayed for you, and if it were not for them praying, you wouldn't be a preacher. In some cases this may be true. However, those of you who became preachers after you had children, I have news for you. It was your child's innocent prayers that put you and kept you there.

Remember, those children you neglect are the same ones keeping your secrets and not telling the church body how you really are, and how you really act at home. Before you begin your tenure in the pulpit, you need to get a particular verse of scripture tattooed on your heart and down in your soul.

"He must manage his own family well and see that his children obey him with proper respect. (If anyone does not know how to manage his own family, how can he take care of God's church?)." Timothy 3:4,5. NIV.

Larry L. Stevenson

THE SINGLE PARENT EPIDEMIC

Boys, men, and men of GOD, no matter what you've been taught it is *not* cool to sleep with every woman you can or every woman that wants you. It is *not* cool to make a baby and decide it isn't your responsibility to take care of the child because you don't have any feelings for the mother that go past your zipper.

I've watched generation after generation have babies, and the then fathers leave the mother to raise the child alone, as if she was Mary and conceived by herself. Remember, Joseph stayed! So what is your excuse for leaving something made by you? For the life of me, I cannot figure out this unwritten rule: a man and woman make a child, the man leaves, and the woman takes care of the child. Somebody please help me with this, because I must have slept through that class. To me this scenario has played out far too often. Answer this example: If my woman and I build a house together, each contributing the same amount of money and time, and when the house is finished she moves in nine months before I do, does this make the house more hers then it is ours or mine? No.

Somehow people think because the woman carries a child in her body for nine months she's the only one with responsibility for it. This occupancy does not give either party the right or the knowledge to handle the responsibility by themselves.

Ladies, I know you're strong. You may have a good job and think you don't need a man for anything. Let me stop you right there and just say, "Yes, you do need a man for something. You need him to help teach that child the other side of life." Nobody said you have to continue living with him or sleeping with him in order for him to be part of your life and help with your child. I know some of you may fear losing your man or woman if you don't sleep with them. But just to set the record straight: If he or she is truly bone of your bone and flesh of your flesh (Genesis 2:23) then no amount of sex, person or devil in hell can keep you from them. If that person is your bone you don't have to worry about losing them, they don't fit anywhere else but by your side, there has never been a rib transplant, one size doesn't fit all. That person should respect your views and values and be willing to come into agreement with you and wait until you say "I DO"

However, you need to understand a few things before you bring someone into your child's life to help you raise your child:

You must trust that person with your life. If you don't trust him with your life, you can't trust them with your child's life. Asking this question *before* you have sex with someone would not only help in the epidemic of single parenting, it would also help erase the epidemic of Aids, herpes and other sexually transmitted disease that affect our way of life. It could literally save the lives of you and your child.

You must seek to know the heart and mind of the person, paying more attention to what's inside than outside appearances, including age or color. External things can tell you a lot, but you can't judge a book by its cover. You need to speak openly and honestly about who they are inside, and then make sure their outside life lines up with their inside life. Seek wisdom and knowledge.

Be very selective. Your child's life is not a revolving door for men and women to come in and out, whenever you or they feel like it.

You must give them the authority to discipline and create structure. If you don't give them the authority to discipline and create structure, you might as well have bought a puppy or called over a playmate.

For single fathers, you don't have to sleep with every woman who comes into your life in order for her to help you with your child. You should also follow the above guidelines.

Folks, there are many people available as mentors for your children: Godparents, grandparents, uncles, aunts, brothers, sisters etc.

Before we close this chapter, I must mention what's happening around the world today in adopting children. Couples of the same sex, are being allowed to adopt children. Regardless of how much money they have, or how loving they are, a child raised by parents of the same sex is still being raised in a single parent household. Although two different sinks are used, they still have the same plumbing, and the child gets the same water (advice, answers, outlook) from both. The child has a need to be able to go to the well of his or her parents and draw out different kinds of water, some filtered, some unfiltered.

DISCIPLINE & STRUCTURE

Throughout the book we've been talking about discipline and structure in a roundabout way. Let us now tackle it head on.

Not only do we as adults need to discipline our own thoughts, emotions and actions, we also need to discipline our children and provide them with structure to give them a fighting chance at survival. We've all seen the different sides to discipline" the good, the bad and the ugly. I believe discipline is a balancing act. You can give too much but you can also give to little.

You really need to use the right tool for each task of discipline you're faced with. Don't use a hammer to flatten out cotton, and don't use cotton to drive in a nail. Each of these tasks requires a certain tool in order to get the desired effect.

You must take some time, think about your discipline efforts, and ask yourself "Am I disciplining my child or is my child disciplining me?" Have your efforts become predictable, therefore leaving your child programmed that a certain action on their part will produce a certain response from you? For example: A parent warns her son that if he raises his voice at the parent he'll be sent to his room until he can calm down and can be respectful. During the conversation, the child fills challenged, uncomfortable or frustrated and ends up raising his voice to the parent. He gets sent to his room to calm down. Now I ask you—who is being disciplined here? Is it the parent or is it the child? Some might say the parent is disciplining the child by sending him away to calm down and think. On the surface it appears that way, but if we look at little deeper we'll find something very startling. First, the child's room is his refuge, a place where he can go and not be bothered. It's where his games are and everything else he need to feel comfortable. So this parent disciplined her son by giving him something he wanted in the first place, although she was convinced she made the decision to send him to his room. The term calming down is funny, because usually the child isn't upset—they're just looking for a desired response out of you, and they know that raising their voice will upset you. So when you send them to their room it isn't for them to calm down, it's so you can calm down.

Think about in the back of your mind when your child is doing these things. You're probably saying to yourself "I can't believe this child just talked to me like that. If this wasn't my son (daughter) we'd would be rolling in the dirt right about now! If he (she) ever talks to me like that again we're going to have problems." I'm sure there are a few explicit words I left out, but I believe we're on the same page. So who's more upset, you or your child?

The "no raised voices" rule lets your child control the disciplinary process by deciding when the conversation will end. And it usually ends when he begins shouting and you send him to his room where he can watch TV or play with his games, while you continue fuming. You've rewarded him for losing his temper. The alternative to this could be, you not getting upset and sending him to his room but defusing the situation right then and there. Let him know that his tone is unacceptable and by raising his voice his punishment will be more then originally thought. By handling the talk along these lines you as the parent remain in control and you teach him how to defuse a potentially upsetting situation and you teach a valuable lesson in controlling ones temper, because you controlled yours.

When disciplining you must be careful not to go overboard into abuse. Discipline has always been meant to save lives, not to take or ruin lives. I'm going to push the envelope of societal thinking right now and say there are some circumstances in which you should spank, whip, or whatever you want to call it with a belt, rod or as my grandmother would say a switch, to show your love for your child. Now let me back that up with scripture.

"Do not withhold discipline from a child; if you punish him with the rod, he will not die. Punish him with the rod and save his soul from death" NIV Proverbs 23:13-14.

"He who spares the rod hates his son, but he who loves him is careful to discipline him" NIV Proverbs 13:24

"No discipline seems pleasant at the time, but painful. Later on, however, it produces a harvest of righteousness and peace for those who have been trained by it." NIV Hebrews 12:11

This is not giving you the freedom to take out your frustrations on your child, it is not saying that you have to prove you're the boss by having a knock down, drag out fight with them. And it most certainly is not saying that to prove your love you must beat them every time you're faced with an issue that needs correction or structure.

I am saying that in certain situations talking proves nothing and will not correct the problem. They won't learn from their mistakes, because the pleasure of doing what they did outweighed the pain of correction. A lecture tells them they can repeat the same behavior next week, and all they'll face is a long winded speech from you. If they get tired of hearing you talk, all they have to do is raise their voice and you'll send them to their room, resulting in them actually being the ones who control the discipline.

Your child may commit an act of violence or rebellion purposely, as a cry for the need to be disciplined—or should I say *touched.* Although spanking is painful, for some children it's the only physical touch they receive from their parents. And that's better than nothing. Even a painful touch can become rewarding to the child.

We do the same things as adults when we feel our spouse, boy friend or girlfriend is not paying us attention or communicating with us mentally or physically. When this happens, we start an argument (we rebel) in order to get the attention we need. You may laugh or shake your head, but you know it's true (We will discuss this in my next book: "Baby we need to talk because I need to listen").

Remember if you don't discipline your child, you're willingly taking the fun out of being a parent. Without discipline, your children will rebel and leave you focused on controlling them instead of having fun with them. You both end up trying to catch up with the past by correcting the present, treating a symptom, and never finding the root of the problem.

In your disciplining efforts, you must also understand that you're raising children, not robots or soldiers; your house is not a sterile environment with strategically placed land minds in it. It's a place where you and your family come together to recharge your batteries, not to have your batteries drained, it's a place where you and or your children should never dread going.

Let us look at structure, something that should begin from day one and continue throughout life. Every word, action, and direction you give your children should have a structured meaning and purpose behind it. When I was a police officer in the K-9/Swat unit, my trainer told me something that took a while to click: "Training never stops. Everything you do is part of training." I don't mean to compare children to suspects out on the streets or police dogs, but let me tie this together: My trainer knew that anything that happened in my life could someday be applied to an actual situation. It's the same for our children. What they learn at home will apply to situations outside the home. Seemingly insignificant things they learn at home will help prepare our children for the world they'll someday face. For example, learning the discipline of homework will later help them hold a job. Helping with chores teaches them how to manage a household.

What your children learn outside the home they will attempt to apply inside the home, and this doesn't always go with the grain of the house. So before something becomes a rule in the house, they must get it okayed by the head of the house. When an officer learns an effective technique out on the streets, he or she must get it passed by the commanding officer before they decide that's how they'll do things from then on. In that way, structure becomes a team effort. Do not be afraid to let your children take part in structuring the house, but don't let them take over.

As a K-9 officer you train your K-9 to search for suspects, drugs, and weapons. At the end of a successful search, you reward them with their favorite toy or lots of praise. Each time they're out on the streets, they're motivated by the reward, but they also understand that in order to receive that reward they must follow your structure (verbal/physical commands and corrections. If you take a trained police dog, unleash him, and let him roam the community it's an accident waiting to happen. Take that same police dog to the same community and direct him, keep him focused, and reward him, and he will be an asset.

A child without structure is an accident waiting to happen, but a child with continued structure who's rewarded (praised) for doing well and corrected for doing wrong is not only an asset, but a joy to be around. You should be so bold and humble as to ask your child whether he or she feels they're being raised as an asset or a liability to society.

We as adults often get busy and high-minded. Before we know it, we're asking our children to handle things they may think they can manage, but their minds aren't equipped for. We must stop asking our children to make adult decisions.

"The rod of correction imparts wisdom but a child left to himself disgraces his mother" NIV Proverbs 29:15

Conclusion

Conclusions always strike me as funny, because they symbolizes the end of something. Although you've read to the end of this book, it's actually just the beginning. Teen violence is on the rise and is spreading faster then an infectious disease. We as adults need to wake up and grow up. We only have tonight to do it, because the Bible says that joy comes in the morning. This has nothing to do with the time of day—it has everything to do with your state of mind. Wake up!

JOURNAL / NOTES

JOURNAL / NOTES

JOURNAL / NOTES

JOURNAL / NOTES

JOURNAL / NOTES

JOURNAL / NOTES

JOURNAL / NOTES

JOURNAL / NOTES

JOURNAL / NOTES

JOURNAL / NOTES

JOURNAL / NOTES

JOURNAL / NOTES

JOURNAL / NOTES

JOURNAL / NOTES

JOURNAL / NOTES

JOURNAL / NOTES

JOURNAL / NOTES

JOURNAL / NOTES

JOURNAL / NOTES

JOURNAL / NOTES

JOURNAL / NOTES

JOURNAL / NOTES

JOURNAL / NOTES

JOURNAL / NOTES

ABOUT THE AUTHOR

Larry L. Stevenson, more affectionately known as "Pastor Larry" is the Servant/CEO of Interpreted Word Ministries. The God given vision for his ministry is to live, speak, teach and know the truth through the incorruptible word of God. Pastor Larry is a humble, uplifting, charismatic man of God, who says, "I've always had a servant's heart." As we look at his past profession as a police officer, and his calling as a preacher. We see this to be very true. In both professions he was called to "Serve and Protect"

Larry is married to his spiritual advisor and best friend Tracey and has two fine sons, Donavon and Anthony. They live in Denver, Colorado.

Invite Larry to speak at your next meeting,

conference or special event.

e-mail: iwministries@msn.com

www.ingramcontent.com/pod-product-compliance
Lightning Source LLC
Chambersburg PA
CBHW031315060726
47590CB00003B/1224